No. T0004

No. T0008

No T0006-B

No. T0005

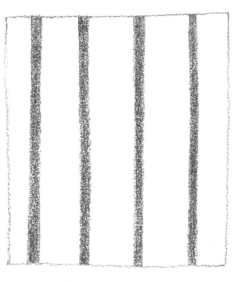

the Ticking

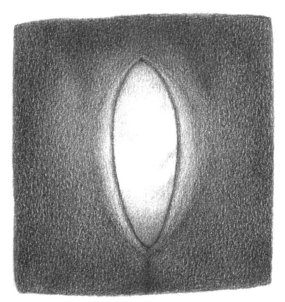

Edison Steelhead was born
on the kitchen floor.

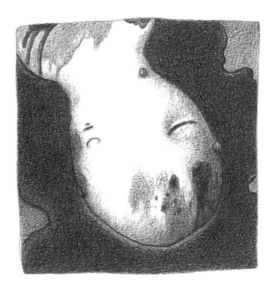

His mother did not survive him.

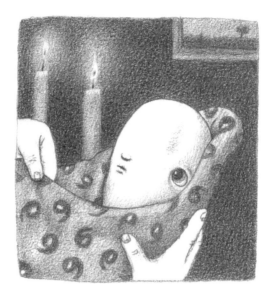

You have my face.

So we'll go away.

Where nobody can see it.

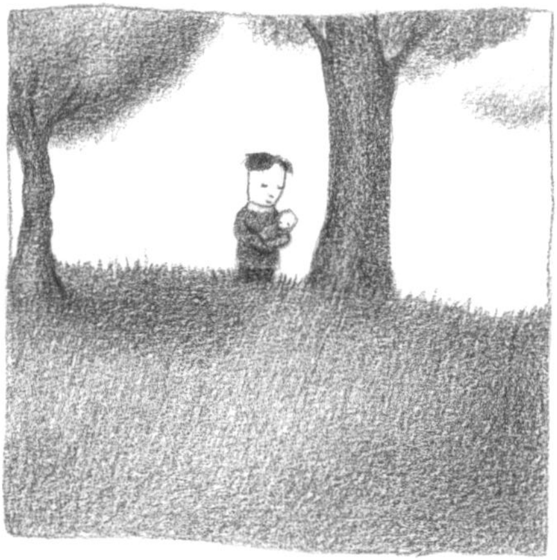

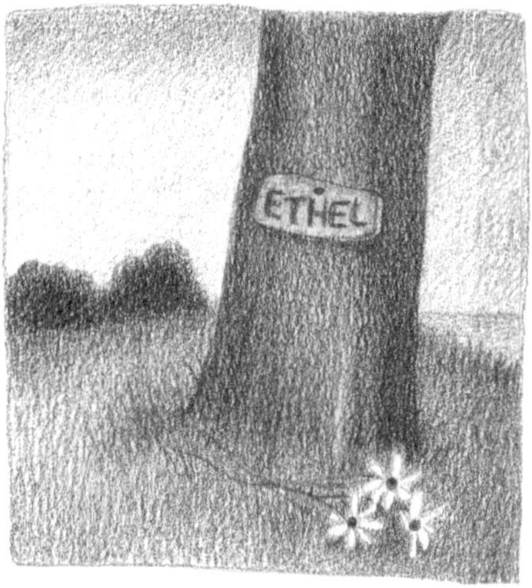
ETHEL

... and fine particles of
volcanic glass ...

...curious assembly of wheels and
gears and axles...

Years later...

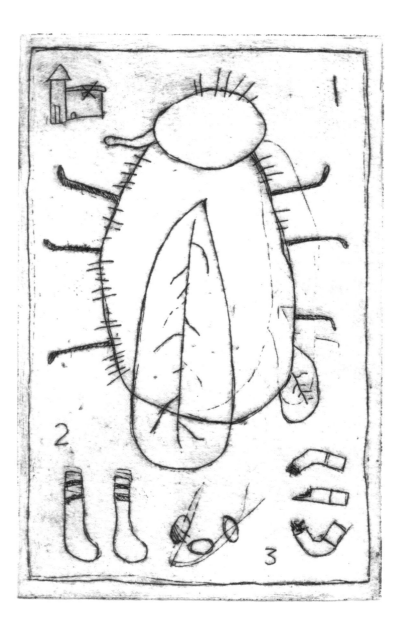

In the sitting room...

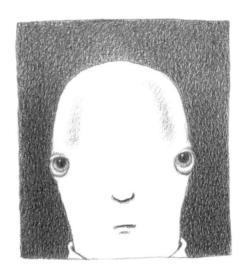

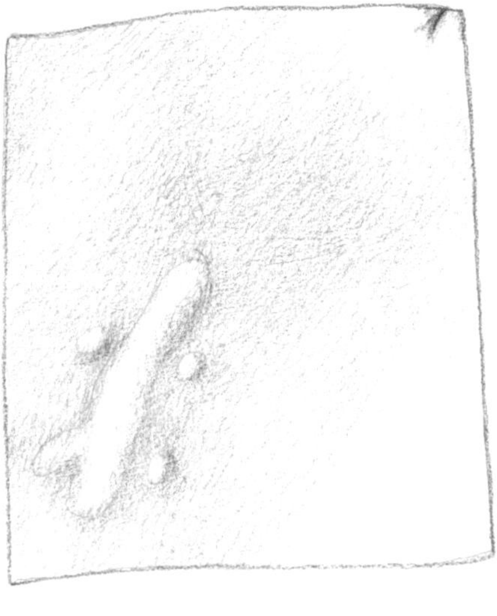

Please wash your hands
before dinner, OK?

Dad, what are those scars on your face?

Eat your meat, Edison.

After dinner...

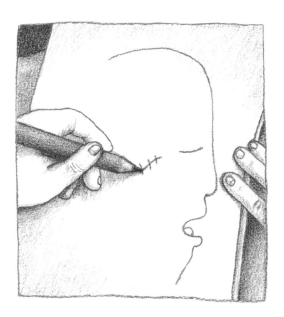

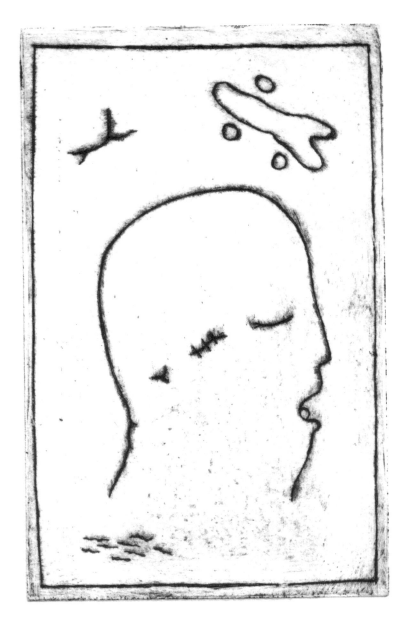

I made this for you, dad.

EDISON STEELHEAD! LAND HO!

Dad!

A boat!

Ed, please cover yourself.

Maybe he brought some nice meat.
We can make sandwiches.

And maybe geoducks.

Dad, did he bring geoducks?
I don't know, why don't you ask him?

SORRY I'M LATE, CAL.

No problem. Come on up to the
house for a drink.

I'D LOVE ONE. BUT FIRST, GEODUCKS FOR EDDIE.

Thank you, Mr. Lauder.

Later...

Edison, it's time for bed.

OK, Dad.

I SHOULD GET GOING, CAL. SEE
YOU NEXT TIME, ED.

Goodnight, Mr. Lauder.

GOOD NIGHT, ED.

Good night, Dad.

Hi.

He didn't like the drawing.

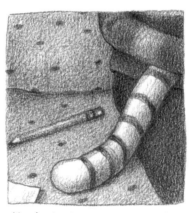

He hated it so much he
threw it away.

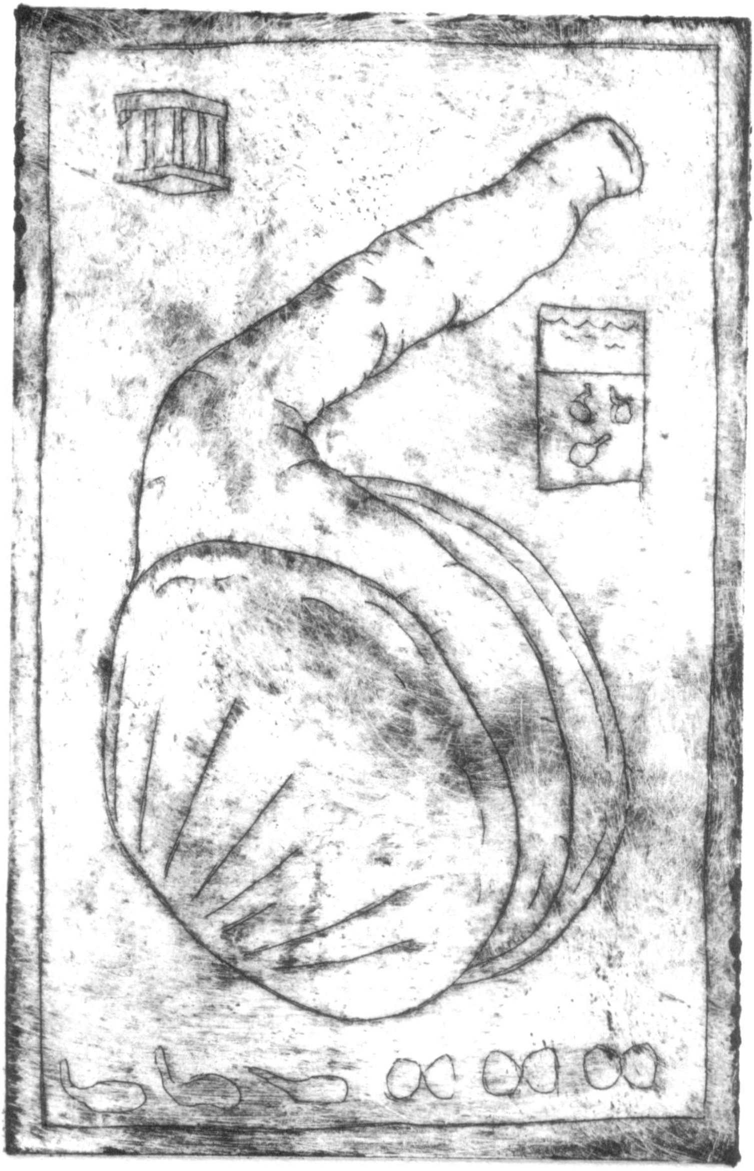

...die Sprache nicht sprechen, lesen oder
verstehen können, oder die grafischen
Darstellungen...

One morning...

It's your mother's birthday.

She would have wanted you to have these.

Tweezers!

Take good care of them.

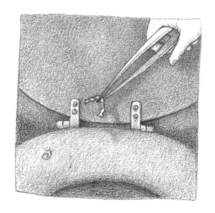

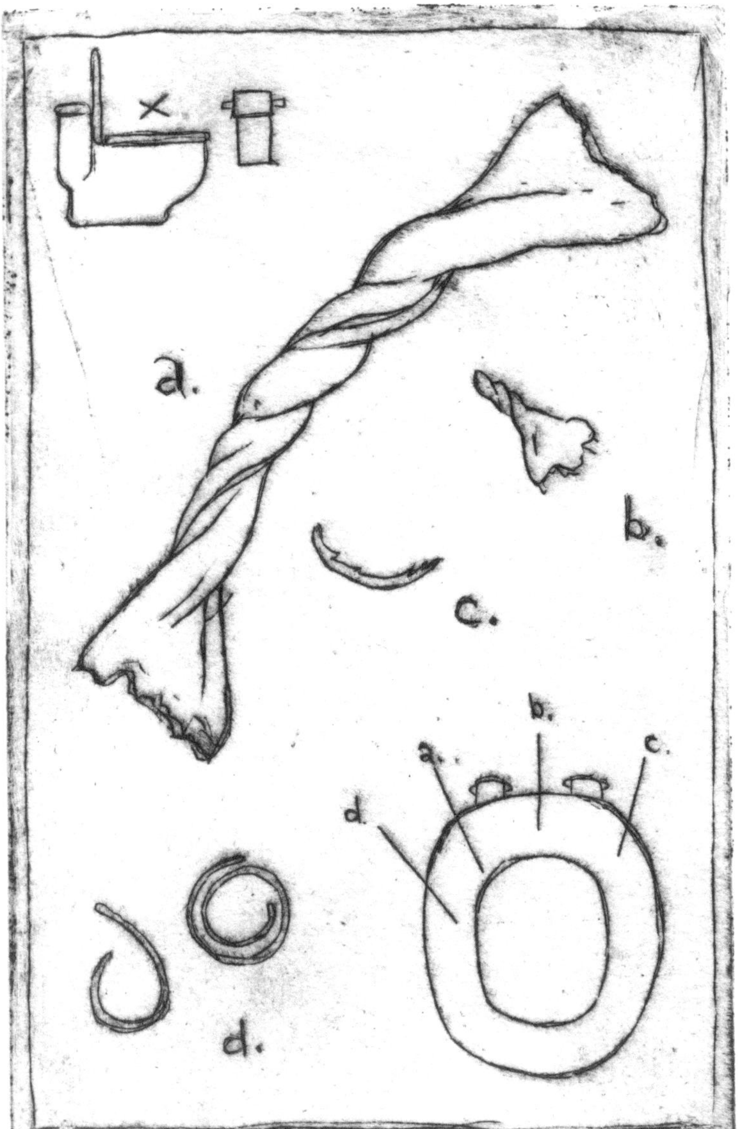

x
a.
b.
c.
b.
a.
c.
d.
d.

What are those lights, Dad?

Houses.

At sunrise...

Do you have your toothbrush?

Yes, Dad.

Don't be scared.

I'm not.

Can you hold it?
We're almost to the hotel.

Can we walk around outside?

Maybe tomorrow after your appointment.

What would you like for dinner, Edison? I'll call room service.

In the morning...

Sit up, please.

WELL, HELLO,

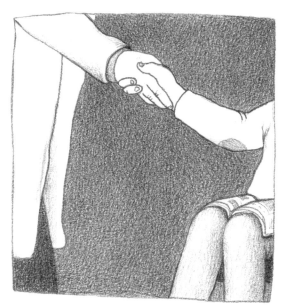

NICE TO SEE YOU AGAIN, CAL.

YOU'RE LOOKING WELL.

AND HELLO TO YOU, YOUNG MAN.

YOU MUST BE EDISON.

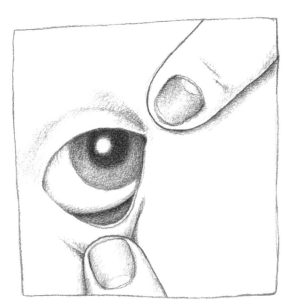

I'M DOCTOR LAMB.

I'M GLAD YOU BROUGHT HIM IN, CAL.

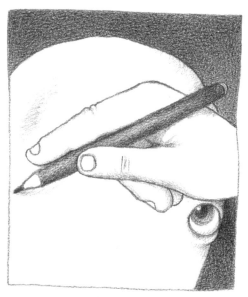

NOW EDISON, I'M JUST GOING TO MAKE SOME MARKS ON YOUR FACE.

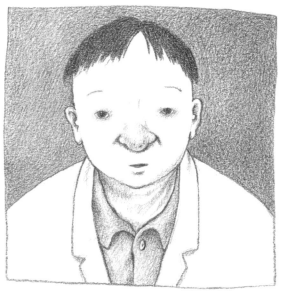

IT WON'T HURT.

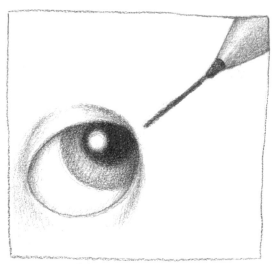

THERE WE GO...

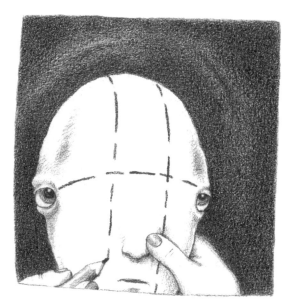

...ALMOST FINISHED.

Hold still for the doctor, Ed.

WE COULD CREATE SOME SOCKETS HERE.

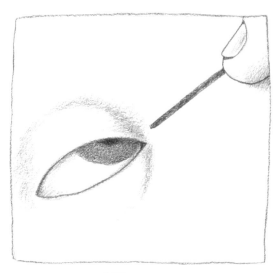

.. AND HERE .

I'D LIKE TO START SOONER
RATHER THAN LATER .

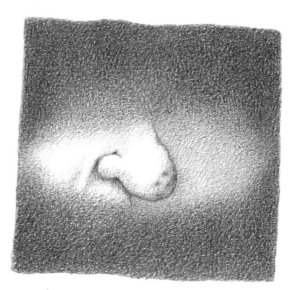

WE'D HAVE AN EASIER TIME OF IT...

SENSITIVE BOY.

Uh huh.

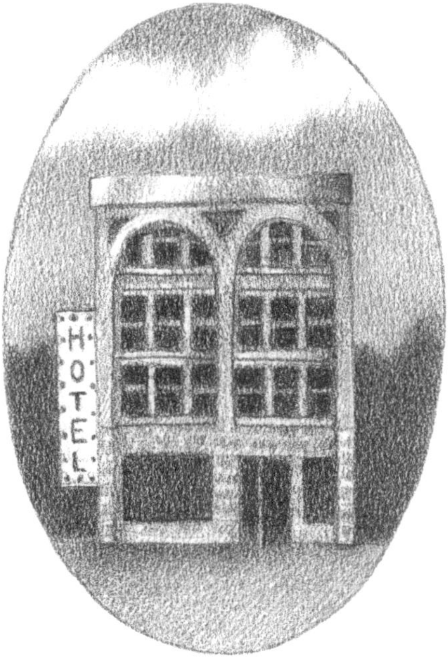
HOTEL

Dad?

I don't want an operation.

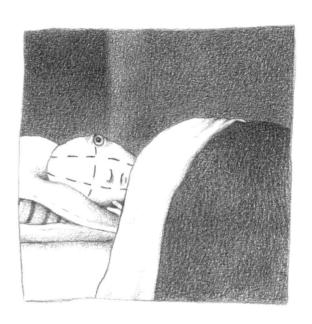

Maybe when you're older.

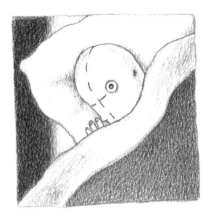

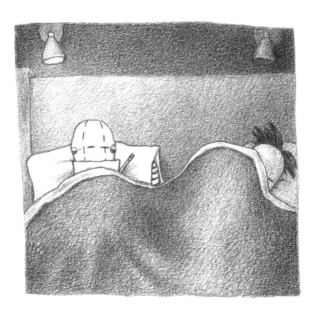

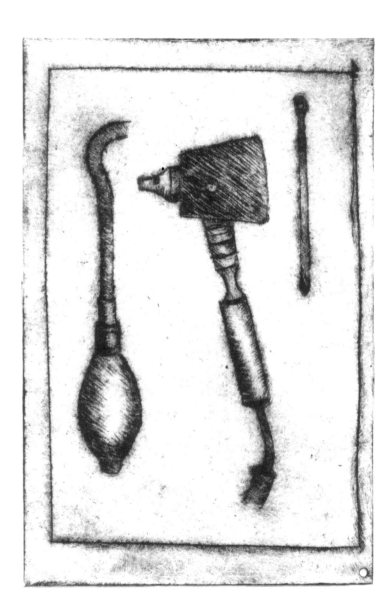

Before sunrise...

How's it going?

Good morning.

I've got someone for you to meet.

Your new sister...

Patrice,

Go on, give her a hug.

There see, she likes you.

I'll leave you two to get acquainted.

Dad?

Nevermind.

Fine.

One day I'll just leave.

And nobody will ever notice.

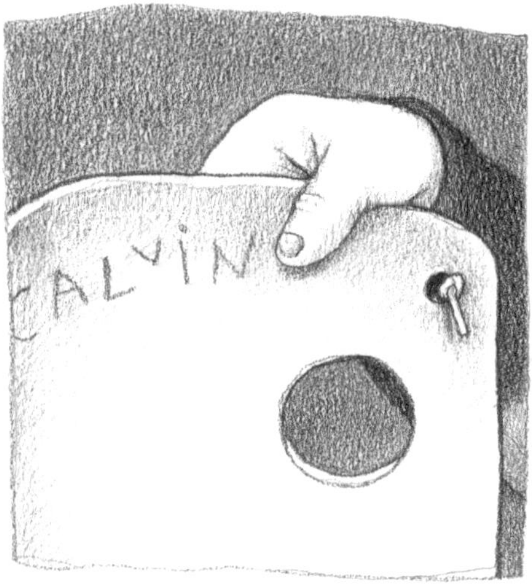
CALVIN

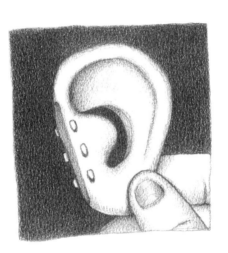

I found these outside.

Is this yours?

Give it to me please... and the box.

Sorry.

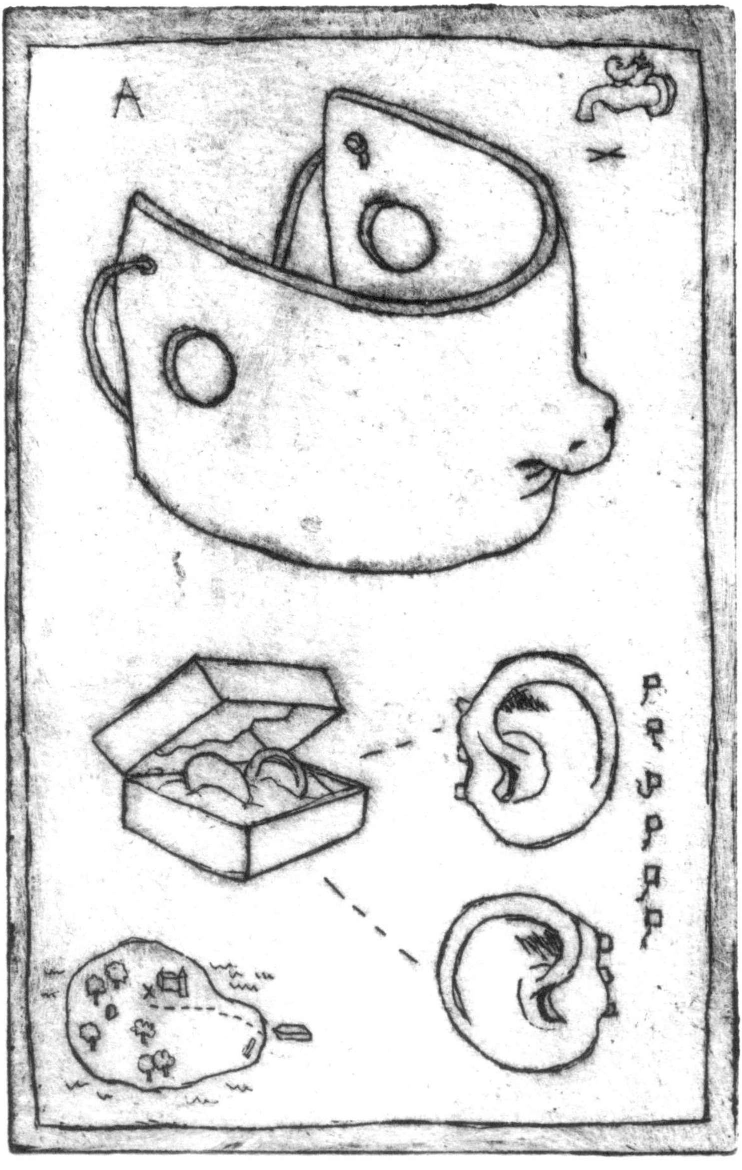
A

... San Marino, Singapore, Slovenia ...

Sometimes I find some good samples over here.

Hey, this is the fly I was
telling you about.

No Patrice!

Is that your answer to everything?
Oh this looks interesting, I think
I'll eat it.

You're so stupid.
You don't understand anything.

Leave me alone.

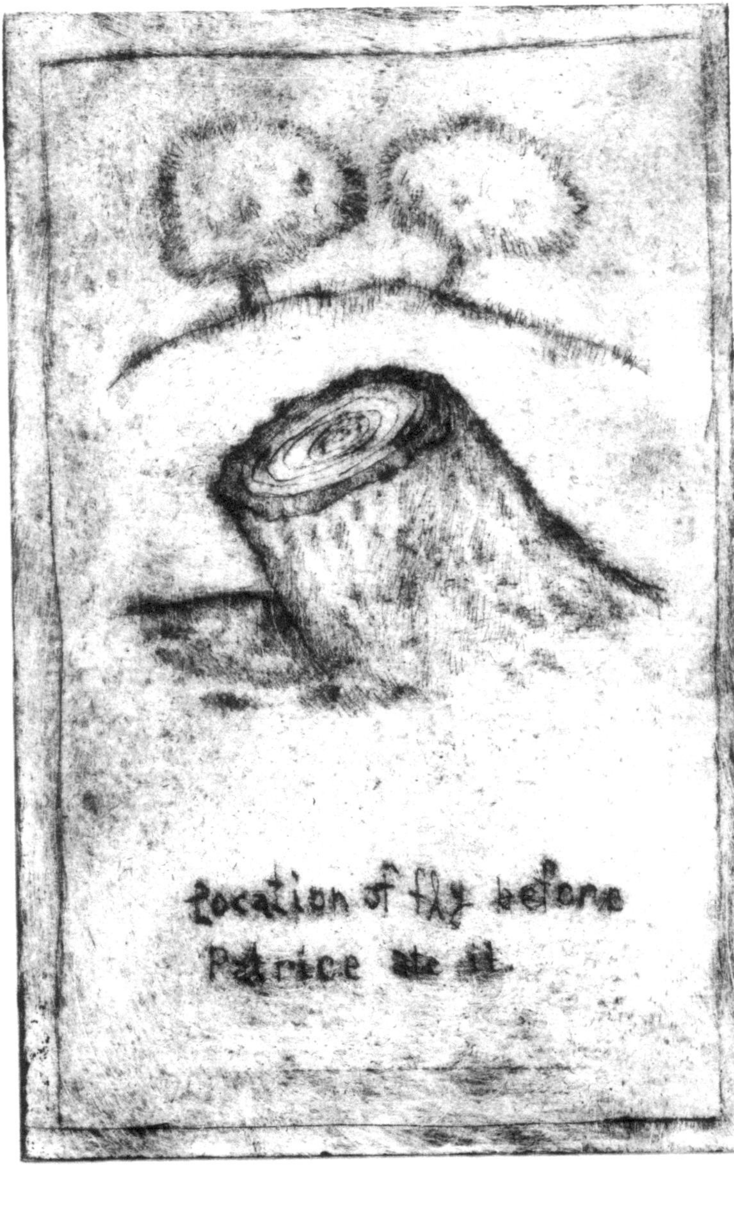
Location of fly before
Patrice ate it.

Don't wiggle your toes.
Just hold still please.

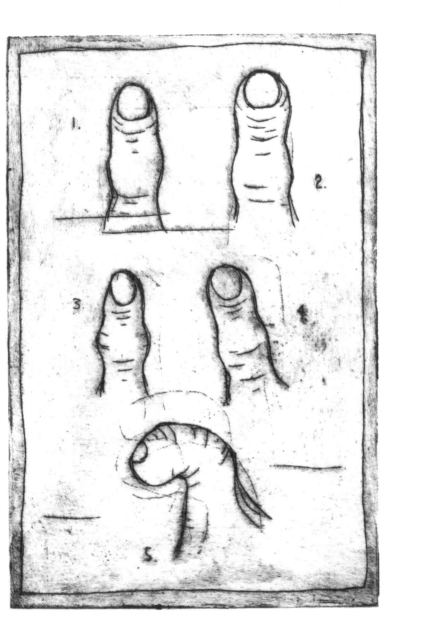

Years later...

Goodbye.

David W. Lamb, M.D.
Plastic Surgery
Roskoland Medical Center

Mr. Calvin
Lighthou

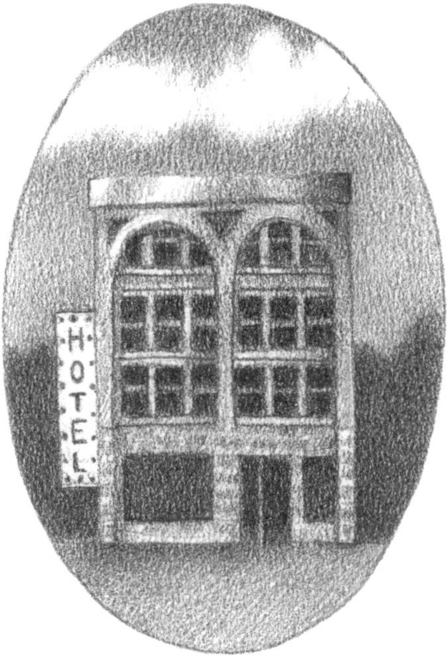
HOTEL

Could you please send me up some spaghetti and a coke.

ROOM SERVICE.

HELLO?

Just a minute.

SHOULD I LEAVE IT AT
THE DOOR, SIR?

No, no thanks.

Could you put it on the bed please.
SURE, HAVE A NICE EVENING, SIR.

Thank you.

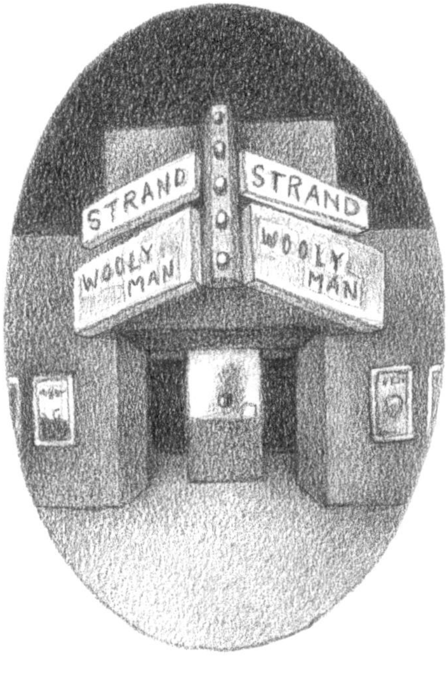
STRAND
STRAND
WOOLY MAN
WOOLY MAN

A week later.

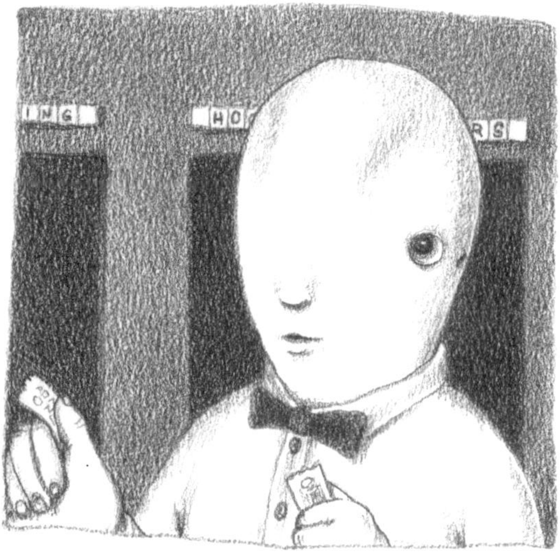
ING
HO
RS

Enjoy the show, sir.

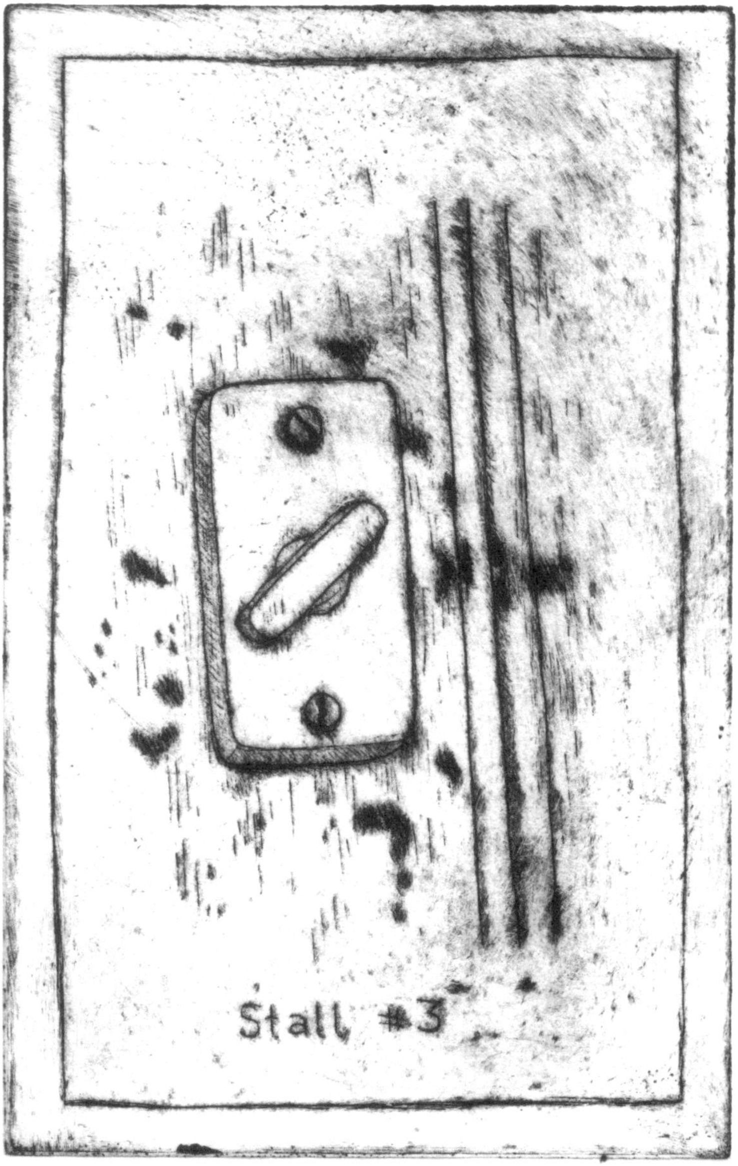
Stall #3

A year later...

OUT OF TOWN

Calvin Steelhead
Lighthouse
Steelhead Island

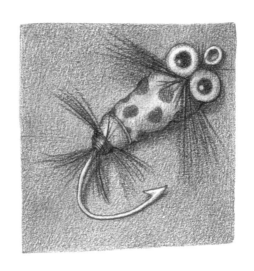

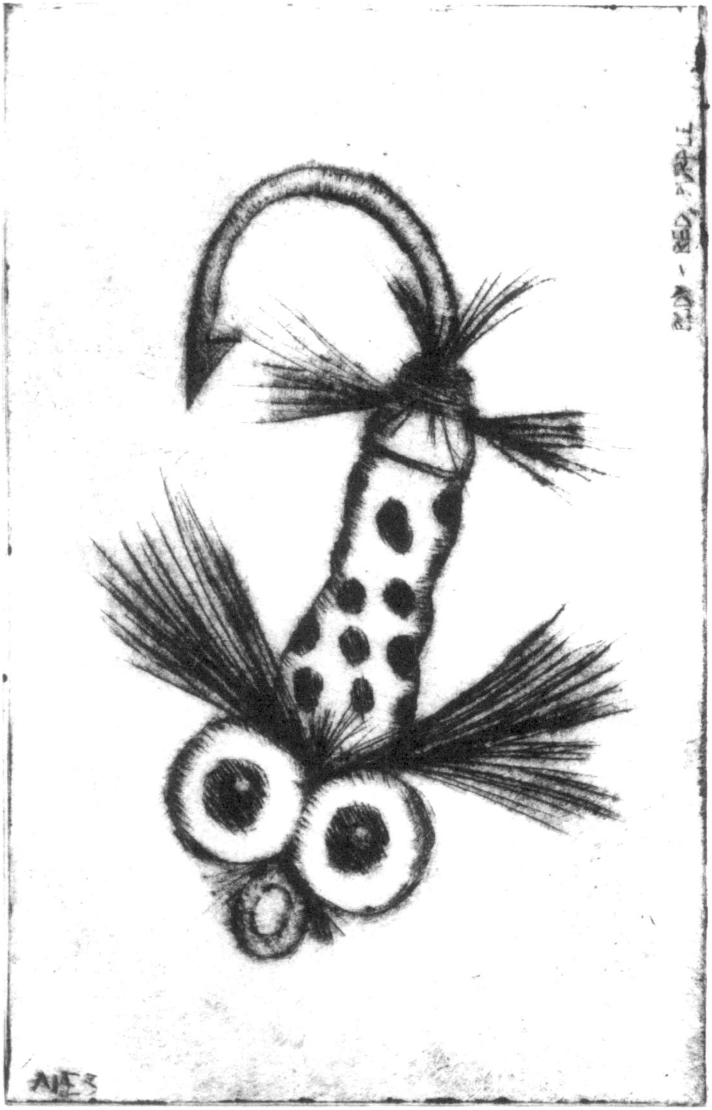
BODY - RED, PURPLE

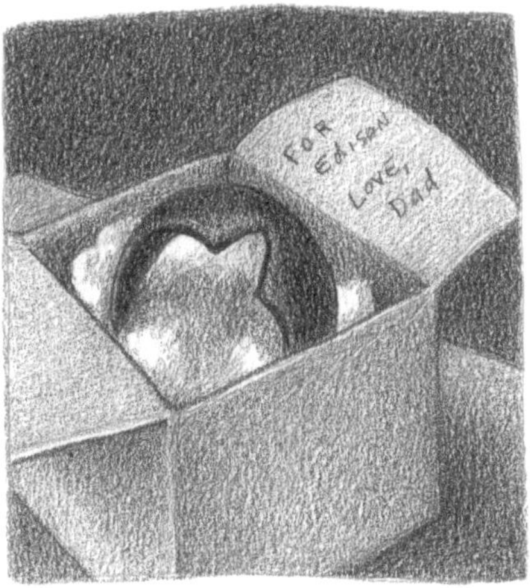
FOR Edison
Love, Dad

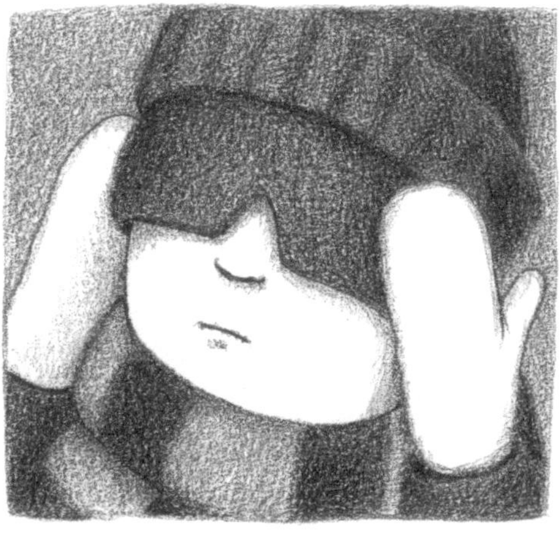

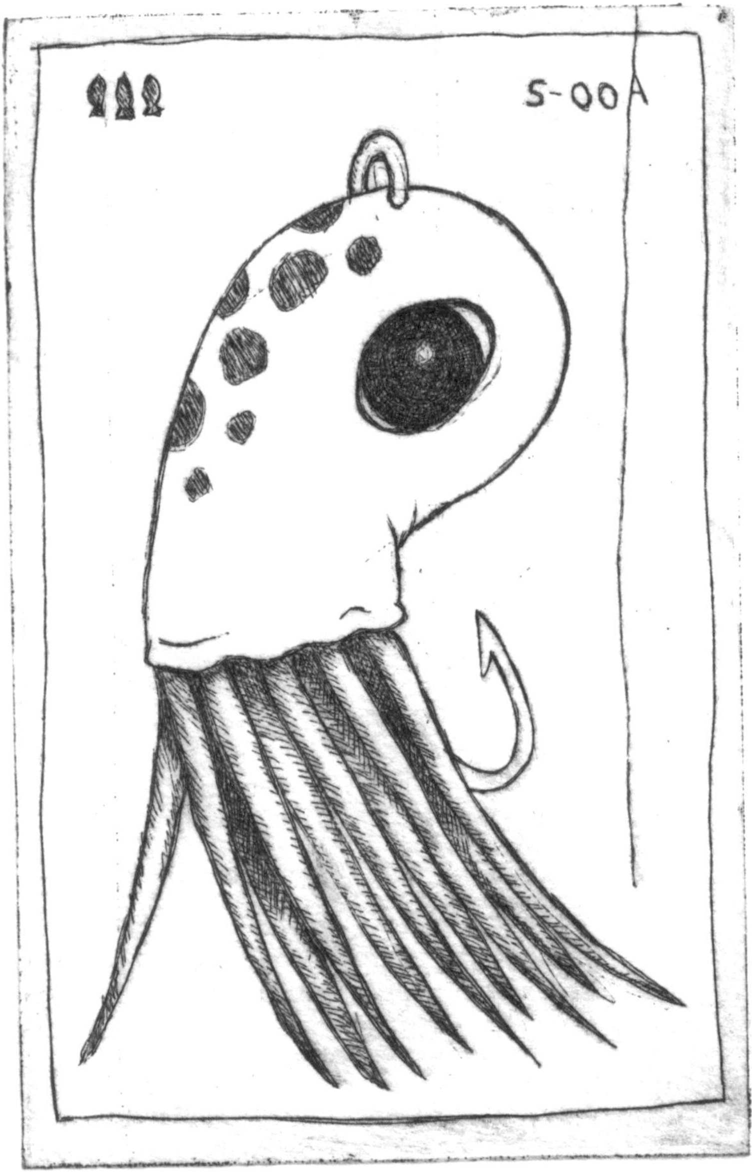
5-00A

THE FLIES. THE FLIES.

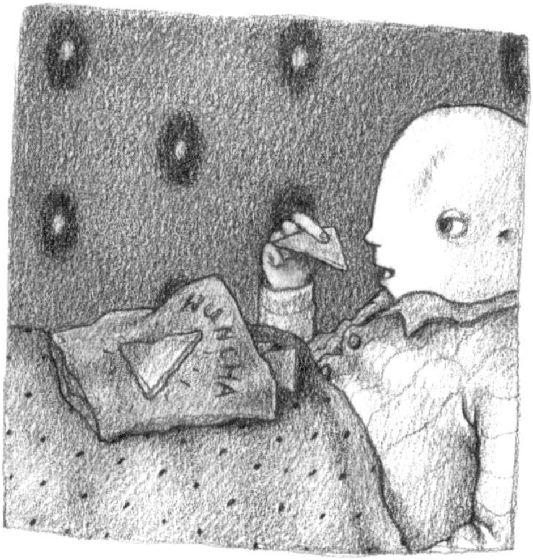
MUNCHA

How did you get here?

Do you even have a face under there?

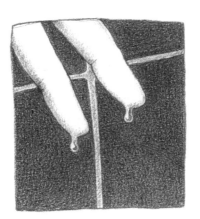

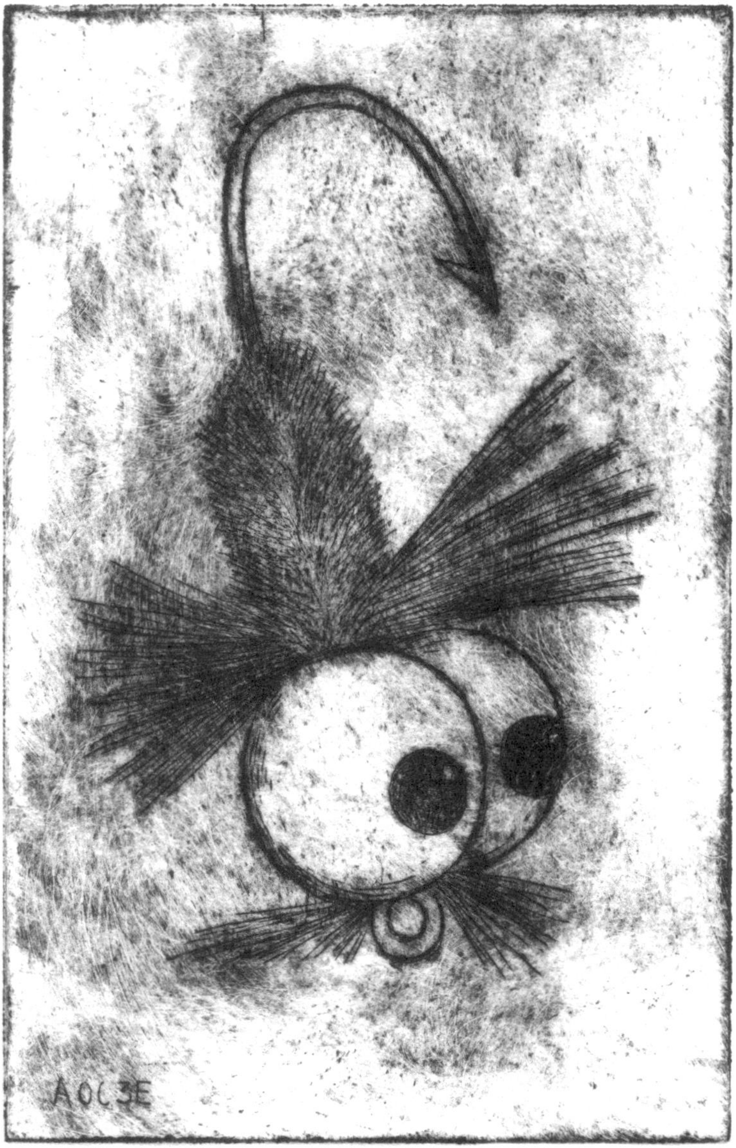
AOC3E

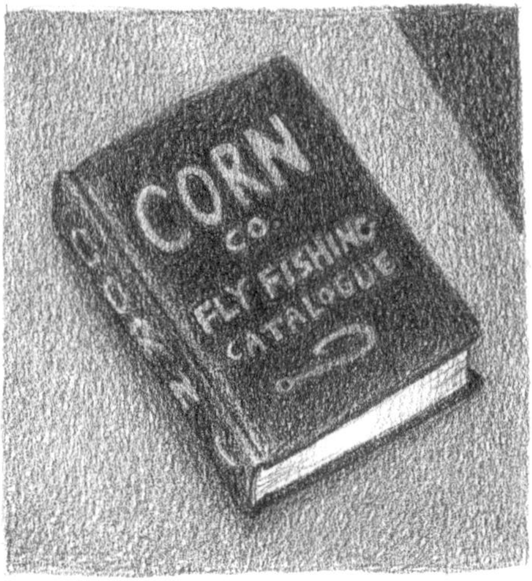
CORN
CO.
FLY FISHING
CATALOGUE

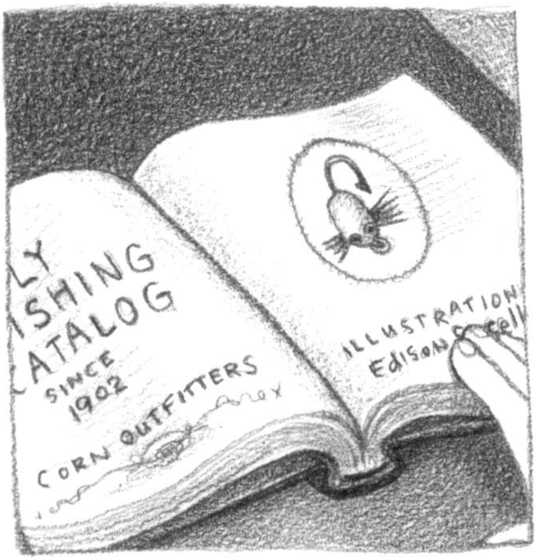
LY
ISHING
ATALOG
SINCE
1902
CORN OUTFITTERS
ILLUSTRATION
Edison

Illustrations by Edison Steelhead.

Huh ?

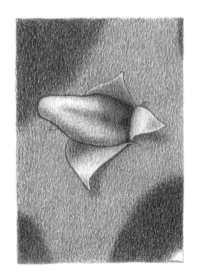

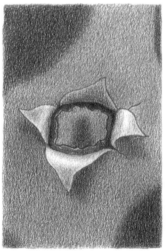

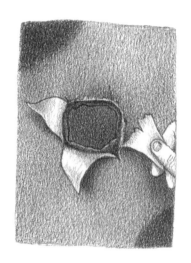

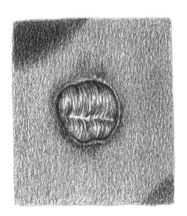

What ?

CALVIN STEELHEAD

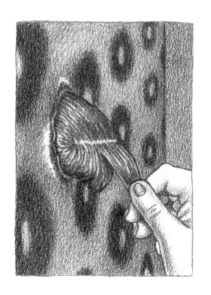

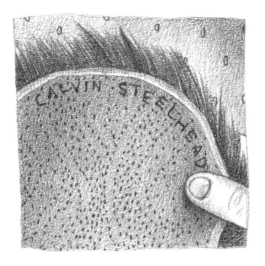

Dad?

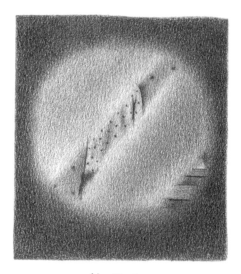

Hello?

Hello?

Dad?

Patrice.

What happened?

What was he doing here?

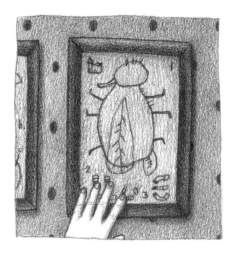

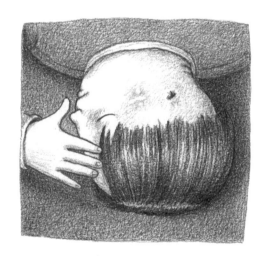

There you go.

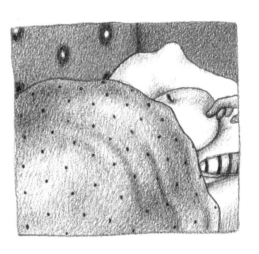

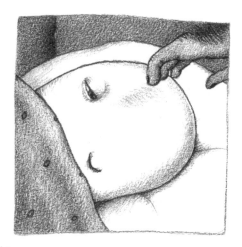

Huh... just a few more hours. Ok?

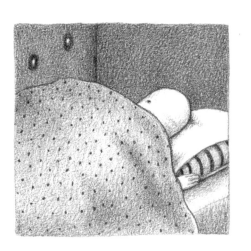

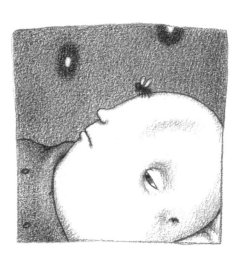

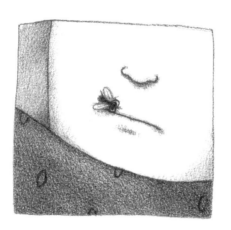

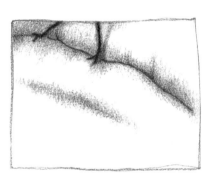

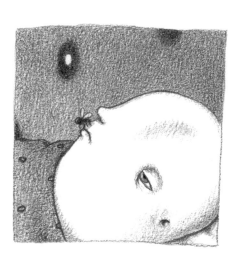

NO! Patrice! Spit it out!

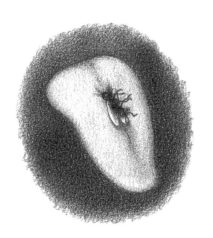

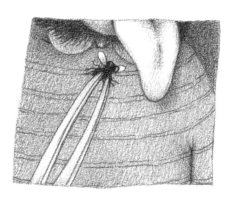

Thank you.

Nice catch.

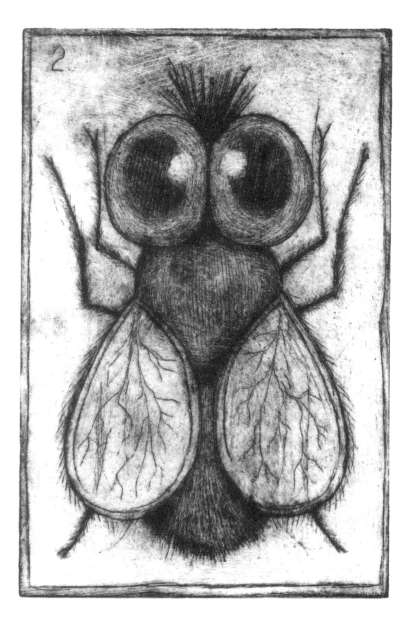

The end.

Also by Renée French
Marbles in My Underpants
The Soap Lady

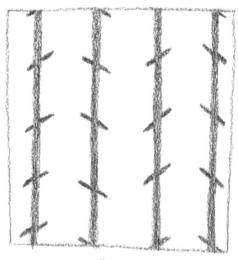

No. T0007

Thank you

Oliver Broudy, Jordan Crane, Jamie
Rich, Scott Teplin, James Gunn,
J.C. Menu, Myla Goedberg, Dani Stockdale,
Colin Summers, Suzy Cline, Lil & Bill
Gladding, Dave Cooper, Ted Stearn,
Jeffrey Brown, Lark Pien, Penn Jillette,
Sammy Harkham, Svein Nyhus, Anke
Feuchtenberger, Brett & Chris, Ann Bobco,
Lisa Rosko, Paul Provenza, Charlie Manlove,
Sean Tejaratchi, Patty DeFrank,
Tom Spurgeon, Dean Cameron,
And Special Thanks to Rob Pike.

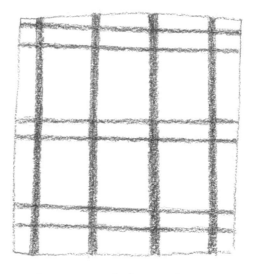

An exerpt of this book
initially appeared in
issue number 171 of
The Paris Review. Book
design by Jordan Crane.
Printed in Singapore.
Second Printing

ISBN 978-1-891830-70-9

1. Graphic Novels
2. Deformities
3. Fiction

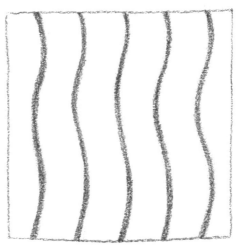

The Ticking © 2005 Renée French.
Published by Top Shelf Productions,
PO Box 1282, Marietta, GA 30061-1282
USA. Publishers: Brett Warnock &
Chris Staros. Top Shelf Productions, Inc.
All Rights Reserved. No part of this
publication may be reproduced without
permission, except for small excerpts
for purposes of review, Visit our online
catolog at www.topshelfcomix.com.

No. T0009